JUNIPERO SERRA

God's Pioneer

TERI MARTINI

Paulist *Press*
New York/Mahwah

Cover art and inside illustrations by Kevin Novack, C.S.P.

Originally published in 1959 by St. Anthony Guild Press; then titled: *Sandals on the Golden Highway,* copyright 1987 by Teri Martini. Revised edition copyright © 1989 by Teri Martini.

Library of Congress Cataloging-in-Publication Data

Martini, Teri.
    Junipero Serra, God's pioneer/Teri Martini.
        p.   cm.
    Rev. ed. of: Sandals on the golden highway. 1959.
    Includes bibliographical references.
    ISBN 0-8091-6589-9
    1. Serra, Junipero, 1713–1784—Juvenile
literature.   2. Explorers—California—Biography—Juvenile
literature.   3. Explorers—Spain—Biography—Juvenile
literature.   4. Franciscans—California—Biography—
Juvenile literature.   5. California—History—To 1846—
Juvenile literature.   I. Martini, Teri. Sandals on the golden
highway.   II. Title.
F864.S44M36   1989
979.4′02′092—dc20
[B]   89-36885
                                                          CIP

Published by Paulist Press
997 Macarthur Boulevard
Mahwah, NJ 07430

Printed and bound in the
United States of America

Contents

Dedication

For My Niece and Nephew, Wendy and Michael Towle

Acknowledgments

I wish to thank my friend and student Carol J. Schlueter of Orange, California, for her assistance in researching information for this book. The contributions of Sibylle Zemitis of the California State Library in Sacramento, California, and of George M. White, Architect of the Capitol in Washington, D.C., were greatly appreciated and added to my understanding of Padre Serra's place in both local and national history.

Sources

The incidents narrated in this book are based on authentic accounts of the life of Padre Junipero Serra.

Historical Memoirs of New California by Fray Francisco Palou, edited by Herbert E. Bolton, University of California Press, Berkeley, California.

Palou's Life of Junipero Serra, translated and annotated by Maynard J. Geiger, O.F.M., Academy of American Franciscan History, Washington, D.C.

Writings of Junipero Serra, Volumes I, II, and III, edited by Antonine Tibesar, O.F.M., Academy of American Franciscan History, Washington, D.C.

The Last of the Conquistadors, Junipero Serra, by Omer Englebert, translated from the French by Katherine Woods, Harcourt, Brace and Company, New York, 1954.

1. Miguel Learns a Lesson

Miguel Serra stood quietly as the stern priest rearranged some papers on his desk. Even though Miguel's heart was beating wildly with excitement, he did not move. He wanted to make a good impression. What this priest thought of him was very important. This priest was the Father Provincial, the head of all the Franciscan priests on this island off the coast of Spain.

At last the priest looked up.

"So you want to become a Franciscan," he said. "This is not an easy thing to do. A Franciscan follows the rules set down by St. Francis when he first started this group of brothers and priests. Being a Franciscan means hard work."

Miguel nodded. His dark eyes flashed with excitement and real desire. He had read many books about St. Francis of Assisi. He knew how St. Francis had given all he had to the poor. He knew how St. Francis loved all of God's creatures. Even the birds and animals knew they were loved and wanted to be near this saint.

The Franciscans lived to do God's work just as St.

Francis had. More than anything else, Miguel wanted to be one of them.

Miguel wished he could say all that was in his heart, but he could not find the words. "Yes, Father," was all he could manage.

As Miguel waited patiently, he suddenly realized that Father looked very angry. Frightened, Miguel wondered what could be wrong.

"Miguel Serra, how old are you?"

Miguel was not surprised by this question. He knew he was unusually small for his age. He was not even five feet tall. He had many scars to show that his size had caused him trouble. Other boys often teased him when he was younger. There were times when he had to defend himself. More than once Miguel had to prove that his size was not a true measure of his courage.

He drew himself up proudly. "I am sixteen," he answered.

The priest's face flushed with exasperation. "Unbelievable!" he said. "What nonsense is this?"

Miguel was horrified. What had he done? He had told the truth. Didn't Father believe him?

"The life of a Franciscan is hard, much too hard for one so young and small as you. Go home to your family, Miguel Serra," Father ordered.

"Go home?" Miguel could hardly believe his ears. He was being sent away. He would not be allowed to become a Franciscan after all. Disappointment settled heavily on his shoulders. Without a word he left the small office. He could not let anyone see the tears that stung his eyes.

He walked through the streets of Palma blindly.

At last he found himself at the waterfront. There the small sailing boats rocked to and fro in the gentle breeze. A clear blue sky smiled upon the island of Majorca. Beyond it the Mediterranean Sea stretched and rippled as far out as the eye could see. Surely this island was one of the most beautiful places in all the world.

How often had Miguel sat here after his day of studying and looked into the distance, thinking of the New World beyond the Mediterranean Sea, beyond the great Atlantic. Sometimes he thought the New World was calling to him and he wondered if he would ever see it.

He wasn't thinking of the New World now. He was too disappointed. There was only one place he wanted to be.

On the waterfront, rising beside the sea, stood the majestic Cathedral of Palma. Miguel hurried inside and threw himself upon his knees before the main altar.

His thoughts turned to his family. As he knelt the walls of the Cathedral seemed to melt away and he saw himself inside the small, white stone house in Petra. Most of the people of Petra were farmers. Like them, the Serras owned farmlands outside the village. But the farmers of Petra liked having close neighbors, and so it was that their houses were side by side along the narrow streets of the village.

Miguel thought of a time several years earlier. He had been lying on his bed. He opened his eyes to find the family at his side.

"Dear Lord, don't let my brother die," his sister Juanna was praying.

"My son, my son!" That was his father, Antonio Serra. "You must get well."

"Hush," said Margarita Serra, Miguel's mother. She put her cool hand on Miguel's burning forehead and smiled. "The fever will go. I know this in my heart. God has chosen my son for His work. Sleep now, Miguel. Tomorrow all will be well."

Miguel closed his eyes. The next morning his fever was gone. Within a few days he was working on his father's farm outside the village again.

But there had not been much time for farming. Miguel studied with the Franciscan priests in the little village of Petra. He studied and he prayed. Finally his family found a way to send him to study in Palma because he had learned all he could at home. After only a short time in the city, he decided to ask the Father Provincial to let him study to become a Franciscan. But now his dream was over because he had been turned down.

Miguel knelt in the Cathedral, thinking and praying. He wondered what would happen next. Had he worked so hard for nothing?

Suddenly Miguel felt a hand on his shoulder. He looked up into the kindly face of an elderly priest. The priest motioned Miguel to follow him. He led the boy outside to the stone steps.

As they left the Cathedral Miguel was surprised to see that it was evening already. He must have been inside a long time.

"I could not help noticing how unhappy you looked," the kindly priest told Miguel. "Would you like to talk about your problem? Perhaps I can help."

Miguel was grateful. He poured out the whole story while the priest listened carefully. "It seems to me," he said, "that there has been some misunderstanding. Let me look into it. I will speak to your friends here in Palma and these priests can speak to Father Provincial. Perhaps then Father Provincial will change his mind about letting you become a Franciscan."

This was certainly logical and the idea did make Miguel feel better. Still, he could not be as confident as his new friend. He need not have worried. Within a few days the Father Provincial asked to see Miguel again.

This time the priest looked at Miguel even more closely than before. He shook his head and sighed.

"Miguel Serra, you are very small for one who has reached the age of sixteen."

"Oh, Father, I will grow. There is still time. I'm sure of it," Miguel insisted.

The priest smiled. He did not look stern at all now. "A man is small only if he is small inside," he said. "The priests who know you best tell me that your faith is strong. It is far more important to grow in your love of God than to grow tall, Miguel. Remember that."

On September 14, 1730, Miguel Jose Serra was dressed for a special ceremony. He wore a rough robe of grayish brown. The robe was fastened at the waist with a rope. On his feet he wore sandals. His head was shaved at the top so only a circle of hair was left.

When the ceremony was over, Miguel was ready to begin his studies with the Franciscans. The Franciscan priests and brothers were known as friars. If Miguel studied hard, he would become a friar too.

A year later, on September 15, 1731, Miguel was ready. In another ceremony he became a Franciscan friar and took a new name. From now on he would be known as Fray Junipero Serra. Fray means brother or friar. Miguel chose to be called Junipero because this was the name of St. Francis' humble companion long ago. Miguel hoped he could be as hardworking and as cheerful as the first Junipero.

Although the new Fray Junipero had not grown much more than five feet, on that day he felt taller than anyone else because his heart was brimming with love for God.

2. *Padre Junipero's Secret*

Junipero Serra had a secret which he kept hidden in his heart. He tried not to think about it too often because then he would want to talk about it with someone else. But there were times when his eyes grew weary of study and he rested them for a while. Then his secret came to mind. God had called him to do special work. He didn't know when and he didn't know how, but someday soon this work would begin.

After joining the Franciscans, Fray Junipero stayed on in Palma and studied to become a priest. During this time, he and his friends went to hear lectures that were given by visiting missionaries.

"Teachers are needed," the missionaries said, "but just as important as teaching is the winning of new souls for God. All over the world there are people who have never even heard about God."

It was then that Fray Junipero knew that God had a special plan for him. Someday he would become a missionary.

In 1737, Fray Junipero became a priest. Now he had the special power, given by Our Lord Himself, to offer Mass. Whatever his hands blessed would be blessed by God. From that time on Junipero was

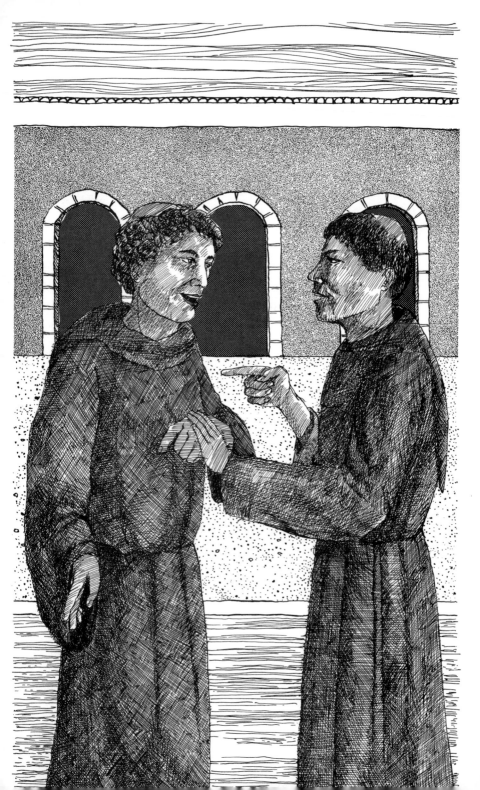

called Padre or Father. Someday he thought he might bless people who had never been blessed before.

Even after he became a priest, Padre Junipero kept his secret wish to become a missionary to himself. He wanted to learn to be a good Franciscan before doing anything more.

He had a brilliant mind. When he was still a young priest, Padre Serra was asked to teach other friars at the college where he himself had studied. While he was there, he made two special friends, Francisco Palou and Juan Crespi.

These two students for the priesthood looked up to Padre Serra. They spent many hours in his company, but not even to them did Padre Serra confide his secret.

As time went on Junipero Serra continued to gain honors for his studies. Many of the older professors thought that Padre Junipero would go far in the Church.

"A mind like his is rare," they said.

"Imagine, a farm boy from Petra might someday become the head of the Franciscans here in Palma. He could be Father Provincial Serra."

"Who knows? He may be the future Bishop of Majorca!" others suggested.

But Padre Junipero was not looking for important positions. He only did the work God gave him as well as he could. Then in 1749, twelve years after he became a priest, the Franciscan Order sent out a call for volunteers to become missionaries in the New World. When Padre Serra heard this, he knew the time had come. God was calling him at last.

He spoke of this to his superiors, but he did not

tell his close friends. Instead, he prayed that God might stir the heart of one of his friends to join him as a companion in his missionary work.

One day Padre Serra walked slowly across the grounds of the college where he was teaching. He admired the beautiful Majorcan day. The trees and buildings stood out sharply in the clear sunshine. He thought of his friend, Francisco Palou, who was now a priest too. He wished that Francisco could share a few hours of this lovely day with him. He hurried to Francisco's room, or his cell, as it was called at the friary, the place where the friars lived.

Francisco was delighted to see him.

"I am so glad you have come. I want to speak to you about an important matter."

Padre Palou hesitated. He seemed excited, but worried too.

"Come, Francisco," encouraged Padre Serra. "We have always been able to speak freely with one another. What is troubling you?"

The young friar smiled. "Not long ago when a call for missionaries to New Spain went out," he confided, "I heard that someone from this province was planning to go. No one seemed to know who it was, but the more I thought about it, the more I felt I wanted to become a missionary too."

Padre Serra was so surprised that he couldn't think of a thing to say. Here was the companion he had longed for. God had answered his prayer.

"I know I have never spoken to you about this, but for some time I have longed to work with those who do not know the Lord and the happiness He can bring," Padre Palou went on. "Now the opportunity has presented itself through work in the foreign missions. I'm only sorry we will have to be separated. I wanted to ask your advice before asking permission to go, though."

There must have been a strange look on Padre Serra's face because his friend stopped talking and then asked if he would like to sit down.

"What is wrong? Don't you feel well?" he asked.

"Feel well?" said Padre Serra. "I feel wonderful. You might have difficulty believing this, Francisco, but I am the one who intends to make this journey to Mexico. Now I find that God has blessed us both with special work."

Padre Serra and Padre Palou were among the first friars from Majorca to volunteer. They wrote to the Commissary General, who was the man in charge of Franciscan missions in the New World. The time for leaving grew closer, but no word came that these two priests had been chosen to go.

Finally the answer came. It was long and formal, but the meaning was simple enough.

"We are sorry that there are already enough volunteers for this trip. We will keep your names in case anyone drops out."

The professors, students and many of the friars were pleased. Now their treasured Padre Serra would stay with them.

Only Padre Juan Crespi was sorry. When he heard of his friends' decision to apply for missionary work, he decided to join them. Now it seemed as if none of them would be going.

Padre Palou was discouraged. "Perhaps we should forget about going," he said.

Padre Serra smiled. "It is God who called us, Francisco. He will find a way for us to go."

During the Lenten season Padre Serra was sent to his own village of Petra to preach. He was happy with this assignment, for he felt that perhaps this would be his last chance to see his family for a very long time.

It was spring in Petra. There was little change in the climate because the weather was always warm and pleasant. Nevertheless, there was the feeling of new life. The grass was greener and the trees had begun to blossom. High overhead, flocks of yellow canaries flew through the clear air.

Padre Junipero was glad to be home again. Everyone was delighted to see this celebrated friend and relative.

"Mama, Papa, how well you look!" Padre Serra exclaimed.

"And you look so strong, Miguel. Surely being a teacher agrees with you," said his mother, smiling proudly.

Padre Serra told everyone how often he thought of his old home in Petra. Then three handsome children came into the room, laughing and excited. When they saw their uncle in his long gray-brown robes, they hung back, suddenly shy. But the shyness vanished as their mother ran forward and hugged Padre Serra.

"Well, you haven't changed since I saw you last," Padre Serra told his sister Juanna. "But who are these three strangers? Surely they are not members of our family. I don't believe they even know me."

With that the children laughed and ran to hug their uncle fondly.

Every day more relatives came to see Padre Serra. He took some quiet walks with his father and his brother-in-law and talked about the farm whenever he had a chance. They discussed the planting of new crops.

Everything he saw and everyone he spoke with seemed more precious to Padre Serra, for he had the feeling that this would be the last time he would see any of them again. Still, he spoke to no one of missionary work in the New World. He loved these people too much to be able to say goodbye to them.

While Padre Serra was in the quiet village of Petra, the city of Cadiz was bustling with activity. There the thirty-three missionaries who had been chosen to go to Mexico were awaiting the arrival of their ship. Five of these Franciscans were men who had never seen the sea. Terrified at the sight of the waves tossing the small ships about, they asked to be excused. They were afraid to make the long journey and felt that they would be of no use as missionaries after all.

To the Commissary General this was a great disappointment. He would have to find men to replace these friars. He came upon the names of Padre Serra and Padre Palou along with three others. He sent for these men.

"You see, Francisco," Padre Serra said when his friend came to tell him the good news, "God found the way."

Because Padre Juan Crespi had volunteered a

little later, his name was not among the five who were chosen.

Padre Serra tried to cheer him up.

"I have a feeling it will not be long before you join us, Juan. I'll pray for you."

On April 13, 1749, Padre Serra left Palma after twenty years there. He set out for Malaga on a small boat with Padre Palou. There they would find the ship that would take them on this great adventure.

Padre Serra was thirty-five years old, yet he had the feeling that his life was just beginning.

3. Trouble on Board

In the seaport of Cadiz the new missionaries waited anxiously for the ship that would take them to Mexico in the New World. Many of these missionaries knew little about the sea except wild and frightening stories. As each day went by, they became more and more nervous.

"I have heard there are terrible storms at sea where the waves become like mountains and sink the ship," one young man told Padre Serra.

"And what about the calms?" asked another. "I have heard that ships sometimes stay in one place for weeks without a breath of wind to move their sails. Then food runs out and the sailors are never heard of again."

Padre Serra tried to calm these fears. He told stories of all the ships that had made safe voyages in spite of everything. The missionaries listened because they were aware that Padre Serra had come from an island village and knew about the sea. But the longer the missionaries had to wait, the harder it was for Padre Serra to keep them from worrying.

While he waited, Padre Serra wrote letters to his

family in Petra. He addressed his letters to a cousin who was the only relative who could read and write. Padre Serra told his parents of his plans and promised to remember everyone daily at Mass no matter where he was.

Finally at the end of August the ship arrived and the missionaries were underway. Fears were forgotten in the excitement of setting out. It was a splendid day. A stiff breeze filled the sails and everyone was eager for adventure.

Padre Serra breathed deeply of the fresh sea air. His chest swelled and his shoulders were drawn back. He stood poised and ready, stretching himself to the full measure of his five feet two inches. And still he felt very small when faced with the enormous expanse of the Atlantic Ocean.

Beside him, Padre Palou chuckled.

"Are you planning to join the gulls?" he asked, nodding toward the birds that circled above.

Padre Serra's eyes twinkled. "Joining the gulls would only bring me back to Cadiz," he answered. "No, I would rather be borne upon the back of a sea monster if it would bring me to the New World sooner, Francisco."

"It appears you have that wish," remarked the younger man, looking about him unhappily. "This ship looks like a monster, an old one."

The ship was not new, and it was filled to overflowing with missionaries bound for Mexico. This did not promise to be a comfortable trip.

Padre Serra refused to let this dampen his spirits. It was a balmy August day, and the wind that whipped the robes about his legs was filling the sails and bringing him closer to the work God had chosen for him.

Padre Serra was a good sailor. He wasn't seasick. When other passengers were, he went about cheering them up. As time went on, it was difficult to be cheerful, though. The food was terrible. Of course, there was no refrigeration in ships in those days. Meat was preserved with salt. The missionaries were usually served dried salt pork.

As if this were not bad enough, drinking water had to be rationed out each day because there wasn't much of it. The water was dirty and slimy. Still, everyone was glad to have it. As the journey grew longer, many people got sick. Padre Palou and Padre Serra did what they could to help them get better.

There were stormy days and days of calm. There was endless work to be done for the sick. Padre Serra never complained or spoke of being afraid. But at night he clasped a crucifix to his heart while he slept.

Hard and dangerous as it was, the journey was not unusually difficult for those days. The ship traveled many miles and reached Puerto Rico safely. Only one night later, they sailed into a terrible storm. Winds howled and giant waves tossed the ship around as if it were a toy. The captain could not hold the ship steady. Finally he told his crew that he was afraid they might never reach Mexico at all because he wasn't sure where they were anymore.

The sad news reached the missionaries who were huddled in their quarters. For the first time Padre Serra felt discouraged.

"Have we come so close only to fail?" he whispered to Padre Palou.

A hush came over the voyagers as they prayed, asking God to allow them to finish their journey safely. In a little while, as suddenly as the storm had come up, it vanished and a calm settled in. Two days later, singing hymns of thanksgiving, the passengers stood on deck as their battered and badly leaking ship limped into the port of Veracruz in Mexico. They had not been lost as the captain first thought. After ninety days of sailing, they were safe at last.

The friars went to a nearby monastery, a place where priests lived and worked together, following special rules to help them do God's work. Many of the friars were too ill and weak to begin the land journey to Mexico City for some time. But after several weeks went by, almost everyone was feeling better. It was time to go on with their adventure. The missionaries were excited. Now they would really see this new land. But there was a problem. How were they to travel?

In imitation of Christ and the apostles, Franciscans went everywhere on foot. This was the rule of St. Francis. Everyone must walk. Horseback riding was forbidden unless someone was too ill to walk. In their own country the friars could observe this rule without much trouble. But here in the New World the distances between settlements or missions were great. It was two hundred and seventy miles from Veracruz to Mexico City. What was to be done? The missionaries turned to Padre Serra.

"I see no real problem," he said. "Those who are

too ill will ride in wagons or on mules. As for myself and my other strong friends," he added, looking around with a twinkle in his eye at Padre Palou and another young priest they had befriended, "we will walk."

Walk! The friars of Veracruz were shocked. "Walk, Padre?" they asked. "Walk two hundred and seventy miles over mountains and deserts in a strange land? No one here observes the rule. It is generally agreed that the rule of walking was not meant for these vast distances. It is impossible to think you can walk under these conditions."

"We will walk," Padre Serra repeated firmly. "St. Francis would not burden the poor animals with his body. We are Franciscans and we will follow his example."

Padre Palou and the other young friar were eager to begin this journey.

Padre Serra teased his new young friend. "Do not become too excited," he said. "Padre Palou and I don't want to lead a sleepwalker to Mexico City. Get a good night's rest."

They were all in high spirits that afternoon, but that night Padre Serra noticed that Padre Palou scarcely touched his food. Coming away from the table, he stumbled and nearly fell.

"Francisco, what is it? Are you ill?" Padre Serra asked, his voice filled with concern.

Between them he and the young friar led Padre Palou to his bed.

"It's nothing," Padre Palou insisted. I'll be fine. It's all the excitement." He laughed. "Perhaps I'll be the sleepwalker you will have to lead to Mexico City."

But that night Padre Palou developed a terrible fever. It was clear he would not be going anywhere for a while at least. He was very disappointed, but he tried to hide this by making jokes.

"Well, you will be happy to learn that your sleepwalker will be doing his sleepwalking right here," he told Padre Serra. "But don't think you can get rid of me so easily. I might be in Mexico City before you, since I will be riding. Who knows?"

Padre Palou looked so pale and forlorn, despite his brave jokes, that Padre Serra could hardly keep the concern from his voice. He thought of the days they had spent planning this trip. He thought of how pleased he was to learn that Francisco would be his companion in the New World. Together they had hoped to begin their first long journey in this new land. And now Francisco was too sick to go.

"Things don't always work out the way we plan. But what has happened is God's will. We shall meet in Mexico City, Francisco."

Sadly the two friends parted. Padre Serra began his long walk. Mexico City was a great distance away, but he would have even farther to walk before his work was finished.

4. The Long Road to Mexico City

The journey to the city started off easily enough. At first Padre Serra and his young companion were able to keep to the road on the plain just outside Veracruz. The country was beautiful. Wild flowers and fruit grew everywhere.

"I don't think I have ever tasted anything so delicious as this fruit," exclaimed the young friar, savoring some berries.

Padre Junipero Serra laughed. "That is what comes of living on a diet of dried salt pork for so many months."

"Perhaps, but doesn't it seem to you that the berries taste especially sweet? And what do you think? Shall we spend the night in the open under the stars? It doesn't seem likely we shall find many people living around here. It would be hard to find anyone to ask for shelter."

Padre Serra chuckled. "The nights will become cooler as we climb higher. Mexico City is seven thousand feet above sea level. You may be very happy to find shelter then. But yes, we can camp in the open tonight."

Padre Serra was right. Mexico was a varied land. The land continually changed from plain to highland to plateau. With it the climate changed from hot to cool and back again. Along the way the friars were fortunate to find villages and sometimes lonely huts. The native Americans were kind and friendly, giving food and shelter as well as directions for the next day's journey. Most of them spoke Spanish because they lived so close to the city where Spaniards lived.

Once the two friars were told they would have to cross a river before reaching a town where they could stay that night. It was already evening when they reached the water, but the river was too wide to cross.

"What can we do?" asked the young padre. "There is not a sign of life in any direction." He pulled his robes more closely about him, for it was becoming cold.

Padre Serra shook his head. "There must be a narrower place nearby. But in which direction?"

The idea of spending the night in the open was not as tempting as it had been at first. They had seen and heard wild animals along the way. Whether or not these animals were dangerous, the friars did not know.

"Let us say a prayer to Our Lord for guidance," suggested Padre Serra.

They had no sooner finished their prayer than they saw a shadowy figure on the other side of the river.

"Am I dreaming or is someone really there?" the young friar asked.

Padre Serra called across the river for help. At

once a man's voice answered. He spoke perfect Spanish.

"What is it you want?"

When he learned their need, the man said, "There is nothing to fear. Walk along the bank until I show you where to cross."

The friars did as they were told. Soon it was too dark to see anything much. They were guided by the man's voice. At last they reached a narrow place in the river where they would be able to cross over easily.

The young friar breathed a long sigh of relief. "How can we thank this man when we do not know who he is?"

At that moment a well-dressed Spaniard stepped into view. He greeted them politely and waved aside their thanks. "Follow me," he said.

He led them to a house quite a distance from the river. Here he offered them food and shelter for the night. He asked no questions and volunteered no information about himself. Padre Serra was puzzled, but grateful for the man's kindness. Had the man come in answer to their prayer?

The next morning they found that a cold rain had fallen during the night and covered the road with ice.

"What a blessing we were given! Surely we would have been very uncomfortable and maybe even become ill if it had not been for this kind gentleman," said the young friar.

Everywhere they went the friars found friends who were kind to them. It wasn't until their journey was almost over that something happened that was to affect Padre Serra for the rest of his life. They had been hungry and thirsty. They had been lost and tired. But nothing terrible had happened to them. It was from a seemingly harmless incident that Padre Serra became ill. While passing through a tropical area, the missionaries were plagued by mosquitoes.

"I have never seen such large insects," exclaimed the younger priest. "They keep me awake with their incessant buzzing all night. And how these bites itch!"

Padre Serra agreed. The insect pests were annoying. For several days a particularly large bite on his leg bothered him. He noticed only that morning that during the night he must have scratched his leg while he slept and it was bleeding. His leg was swollen and a little stiff now. Padre Junipero Serra began to limp. It was becoming harder and harder to keep up with his young friend's loping pace. But he said nothing.

By evening his leg was very sore. But it was December and the friars had only a week's march before reaching the College of San Fernando outside Mexico City. Padre Serra did not intend to stop now.

When they set out the next morning, Padre Serra was pale and unusually quiet. The young priest set a slower pace. Suddenly he stopped.

"What's the matter? I am not so old that we must crawl to the city," Padre Serra joked.

"We are not going to walk or crawl another inch until something is done about you. You are ill, whether you will admit it or not, Padre Serra. We are going to the nearest village until you are well."

Padre Serra was too tired to argue. He followed his young friend. But after a day of rest, his leg was better. He insisted on continuing their journey.

"Very well," said the young friar. "Our friends

here have offered to give us a mule. You can ride and I will walk beside you."

Padre Serra would not hear of it. "I am surprised at you. St. Francis meant us to walk. That was our plan. I can't let a mosquito bite stop me." He spoke gently but his lips were firmly set.

And so it was that on New Year's Day 1750, two dusty travelers arrived at the College of San Fernando. In the distance were the tall church spires of Mexico City.

Padre Palou, who had ridden by coach from Veracruz, was there to greet them with members of the college staff.

"I can hardly believe my eyes," exclaimed the head of the College. "Here they are, just as you said they would be, Padre Palou. Such determination! Such faith! We can all take a lesson from these valiant friars."

"Francisco! How well you look! I am so glad to see you," Padre Serra said.

For a while it seemed that everyone was talking at once. The story of the long journey was told over and over again. It was a joyous occasion. But when Padre Palou noticed Padre Serra's limp, he was upset.

"We must send to the city at once for a doctor."

"Now, Francisco," Padre Serra said, "you are worried about nothing. I am fine. My leg will be better before you know it. Let us hear no more about this. Agreed?"

Padre Palou did not argue, but he looked worried.

"Agreed," he said.

"Fine! Now tell me what you have been doing and what our life will be like here at the college."

The friars stayed at the college for a time to prepare for their work with the native Americans. The missionaries had to learn something about the different tribal groups, their languages and customs. For five months they studied.

Then one day the friars heard that missionaries were needed in a place called Sierra Gorda.

"Would any of you like to work among the people there?" asked the friar who was in charge of missionaries.

At once Padre Serra stepped forward. Padre Palou immediately followed his example as did several others. Eight friars volunteered.

Before they left for this new work, they were given a warning.

"It is only fair to tell you that this will be difficult work. The climate can be hot and uncomfortable. Many of our missionaries have become ill in Sierra Gorda."

But Padre Serra hardly heard the warning. Nothing could dampen his spirits.

"At last," he thought. "This is the moment for which I have waited and prayed."

In a few days Padre Junipero Serra set out with the others on this new journey. Again it was a long walk—two hundred miles to the north. And still it was only the beginning.

5. The Little Missionary of Sierra Gorda

The missions of Sierra Gorda were made up of five wooden churches. Each church was separated from its neighbor by a few miles of rugged, stone-covered land. The missions were nestled in a group of mountains north of Mexico City. The climate here was hot and very damp. It was most unpleasant.

The Spanish soldiers stationed in Sierra Gorda were forever complaining about something. When news that Padre Junipero Serra and some new missionaries were coming to work there, the soldiers at the headquarters in Jalpan were surprised.

"What a mistake!" said one of the soldiers. "These missionaries will not last very long here. Soon they will be begging to go back to Mexico City where the climate is better."

But Padre Serra did not mind the climate. He was anxious to meet the native Americans who lived in Sierra Gorda. These people were members of the Pame tribe.

The first thing Padre Serra did when he arrived was to study the Pame language. It was hard to learn, but little by little he mastered it.

At first it was only the children who showed signs of friendliness. They were delighted by the little lame Friar who made up games and played with them. They loved the stories he told, too.

It was because of one of the stories that the children and Padre Serra began to plan a surprise for the grown-ups at Christmas. The boys and girls were excited.

The Pame children came every day to the mission center at Jalpan. Although their parents were shy about visiting the friars, the children eagerly crowded about Padre Serra. Some leaned against his arm while he talked to them. The children were handsome youngsters with dark hair and large dark eyes.

One little boy, the youngest of the group, insisted upon climbing into the padre's lap. Today Padre Serra was reading them a story about Jesus and his followers, the apostles. He read the story to the children in their language, translating as he went along.

Little Juan wriggled and fidgeted. It seemed like a very long story to him. Juan was really too young to understand the story, but he liked to be near the padre.

What Juan really enjoyed was the surprise they were planning. On Christmas Day the children were going to put on a play. It was about some people with wings who came to show shepherds a new baby.

Juan played the part of the smallest shepherd who brought a little lamb to the baby called Jesus. Juan especially liked this part because Padre Serra told him that when he was a little boy, he had been a shepherd for his father.

Juan wriggled around and looked into the padre's eyes. "Is it time yet?" he asked.

Padre Serra smiled. "Not yet. It will not be long. You must be patient, Juan," he said and went on reading.

Little Juan was disappointed, but he smiled at his friend. He leaned his head against the friar's shoulder and prepared to wait. He liked it when the padre called him by name. It was the padre who had given him this new name.

A few minutes passed but they seemed like hours to Juan. Juan looked at the book that Padre Serra was reading and had an idea.

"If Padre can't read the book, he will have to stop," Juan thought. Suddenly he reached out and covered the pages with his hands. He looked around shyly at the padre from under his dark lashes.

The other children laughed. Padre Serra was trying hard to look stern. "Juan," he said, "if you cannot be patient, we will have to send you away until we are ready to practice our play."

Poor Juan! He did not want to be sent away, but he was tired of waiting. Two large tears ran down his cheeks.

Padre Serra was not really angry with Juan. He smiled an understanding smile. "Well, our story today was rather long," he admitted. "Perhaps we had better finish it tomorrow."

The children were delighted. Now they could practice the play. Amid shouts and laughter they all went off to work on the Christmas surprise.

There were several different classes offered at the mission each day. There were special classes for grown-ups, older children and the little ones. The padres taught about Our Lord and the Catholic Church. They also taught the Pames new farming methods.

At first only a few of the Pame adults came. But soon more people joined the classes. They noticed that with the padres' help their farm crops brought in larger harvests. A group of Pames came to Padre Palou personally to ask advice about new crops. He was excited about this.

"Think how much confidence the Pames are showing in coming to ask advice. I feel we have become friends."

"Yes, we have," Padre Serra agreed. "Francisco, I could not have imagined how happy this work would make me."

His work continued to make him happy and it went well. The surprise play at Christmas was a great success. It helped the Pames to understand the meaning of the birth of Jesus.

After that there were other plays and processions on special feast days. The church at Jalpan was always kept beautifully decorated. More and more of the Pames came to Mass.

Besides farming the Pames wanted to know about new crafts and trades. The friars taught them what they knew. Some taught how to care for sick animals. Some taught how to weave and sew. The little mission was growing.

One day Padre Serra called everyone to the steps of the wooden church.

"More and more people are coming to this little church," he said as he gestured at the small, weather-beaten building. "But see how small our church is! There is hardly enough room for all of us inside."

Everyone agreed. The church was getting crowded. They began to whisper among themselves. Finally one of them said, "Padre, we could build another church. We can get more wood. We can make one bigger than this."

Padre Serra was pleased, but a wooden church was not what he had in mind.

"Why not a church of stone?" he asked. "We have all the stone we need. Such a church will last many more years. It will be a fitting house for God."

Then Padre Serra showed the plans he had drawn up. The church would be much, much bigger. It would be fifty-three yards long and eleven yards wide. It was to have a dome and a bell tower.

Not everyone believed it would be possible to build such a church.

"It will take a long time, but we can do it," Padre Serra said.

The work began at once. Padre Serra and the friars worked with the Pames carrying rocks and hauling sand to make the mortar that would hold the rocks together.

Slowly, very slowly, the church took shape. It was seven years before it was finished.

All the people were proud of the work they had done. The bell tower rose high in the mountain air, pointing toward heaven. The walls were as solid as a fortress. Today this splendid church is still standing, more than two hundred years later.

The people of the other four churches of Sierra

Gorda were inspired by the church at Jalpan. They began building churches too. One of these churches was built at Tilaco. There Padre Juan Crespi had been assigned to work. Just as he promised, he had joined his friends in their missionary work in the New World.

As soon as he could, Padre Serra got an organ installed in the new church. Some of the Pames learned to play it. Soon everyone was singing hymns.

Padre Serra found that the best way to teach about the Catholic Church was through little plays. There were plays at Christmas and plays at Easter. These helped, but one thing bothered him. Some of the Pames still visited their god called Cachum, Mother of the Sun.

High in the mountains, reached by a narrow stone stairway, was the temple of Cachum. It was watched over by an old, old man. Inside the rough wooden building was a statue of Cachum, carved in white stone. It was the image of a woman's face. Here many of the Pames still came to ask special favors. Sometimes they asked Cachum to make the sick people well. Sometimes they prayed for rain. The Pames went to the god when they wished to be married.

Finally Padre Serra spoke to some of the young men. "You must realize that you cannot be real Christians until you give up all gods but the one true God."

As he spoke some of the men seemed uncomfortable, but they said nothing.

"You must decide between Cachum and the true God," Padre Serra told them.

For several days some of the Pames were not seen at the mission. Padre Serra was worried about them. He spent a great deal of time in church praying for them.

Then one day a murmur of excitement swept through the mission. People from the fields came running. Classes stopped. A solemn procession was approaching. Padre Palou sent one of the children to the church for Padre Serra. In a moment he appeared on the steps.

As the procession drew near, everyone gasped in amazement. The missing men had returned. On their shoulders they carried the marble image of Cachum. This they presented to Padre Serra.

"We have chosen, Padre," they said. "None of us will visit Cachum again."

Padre Serra was so happy he could not speak. Later, on a trip to Mexico City, he carried this statue of Cachum to the College of San Fernando as a reminder of the great works God performs through His love.

For eighteen years Padre Serra worked in Sierra Gorda and at the College of San Fernando, training new missionaries. In 1767, he traveled across Mexico to the Gulf of California. Lower California was a peninsula, a long piece of land surrounded on three sides by water. On this peninsula were fifteen missions. Padre Serra was appointed the head of these missions. Padre Palou and Padre Juan Crespi were sent to work with him.

There was much work to be done in these missions. Padre Serra thought he would be there a long time. What he did not know was that plans were being made in Spain and in Mexico City that were to change his entire life.

In Spain alarming news had reached the King.

"Russian ships have been seen along the Pacific coast above Upper California," the King was told. "Perhaps the Russians are thinking of coming down from the northwest where they have claims in Alaska."

This news worried the King of Spain. For some time Russians had been sailing along the American coast hunting the valuable sea otter. Maybe they were getting ready to seize Spanish land.

As early as 1602, a Spanish explorer had anchored at a port in Alta or Upper California. The explorer called this port Monterey, meaning "the King's Hill." He claimed the land for Spain. The land included Upper and Lower California. Now that claim was being threatened. Spain would have to move quickly to protect her land in California. Orders were sent from Spain to the leader in Mexico City. This man was called the Viceroy. The Viceroy made plans to build settlements in Upper California so that the Russians would not try to move in.

"We will send two ships," the Viceroy said. "These ships will carry men and supplies to build forts and settlements. The ships can find the Bay of Monterey and settle there."

"A land expedition should be sent too," said one of the Viceroy's advisors. "Gaspar de Portola is an experienced soldier. He can take charge of both Upper and Lower California. He will keep the land safe for Spain."

The Viceroy agreed. "What is really needed are

permanent settlements in California. We should build missions there the way we have in Mexico and Lower California. I know just the man to build these missions."

Not long afterward Padre Junipero Serra learned that he had been chosen Father President of all the new missions to be built in Upper California.

"What a marvelous opportunity!" he thought. He was to be God's pioneer in this unknown land.

6. A Most Remarkable Priest

In the harbor of La Paz in Lower California a ship rode at anchor. This was the San Carlos. In a few days it would leave to sail to San Diego in Upper California. Later another ship would follow. These ships would bring all the necessary supplies for the new settlements in Upper California, supplies that the land expeditions could not carry.

Commandant Portola, Governor of California, would lead part of the land expedition himself. Padre Serra, the Father President, would be traveling with Portola. From the moment they met, Padre Serra felt that Commandant Portola did not know what to make of him. The commandant seemed suspicious of priests. Padre Serra could tell that the experienced soldier thought the friars would be a burden to him. Perhaps he did not think that building the missions in California was a good idea.

Every time Commandant Portola was around, Padre Serra had the idea that the man was watching him. The little friar was something to see with his robes tucked up about his knees while he worked to finish his packing for the missions. The missionaries would need many vestments for the priests to

wear at Mass and other religious articles for the churches.

Nearby Jose de Galvez, who had been appointed by the King of Spain to organize the entire expedition, worked too. The fine Spanish gentleman had taken off his coat and rolled up his sleeves. He and Padre Serra were having a contest to see who could finish packing first. They were both excited about the adventure of traveling to a new land that few people had even seen.

"Well, you are very slow today," Don Jose de Galvez teased. "If you carry on like this, the ships will never leave."

Padre Serra laughed. "Never fear, sir. I can keep up with you. Just take care that you pack those vestments carefully. We will want them fit for use when we open the mission of San Buenaventura."

Galvez shook his head. "Always looking ahead, Padre. Well, I'm looking ahead too. I'll be at San Buenaventura to see you wearing these vestments, and they'll be in good condition. I know how to pack."

At first the antics of the little friar and Inspector General Galvez caused much comment from the surprised soldiers who were also preparing for this adventure. But now they had become used to the friendly contest.

To begin, there would be three missions. Each mission would be named after a saint. In Spanish "San" meant a male saint and "Santa" meant a female saint. San Diego would be the first mission. Then San Buenaventura would be built to the north. Next a mission would be built at Monterey.

In time Padre Serra hoped there would be a chain of missions lying along the coast of Upper California. In Spanish he called the chain of missions El Camino Real—the Royal Highway. He thought of it as a kind of golden highway dedicated to the King of Kings.

Padre Serra was happy with his great plans for this new land. He paused a moment in his work. "You know, I have been thinking," he told Galvez.

"Well, what have you been thinking? Don't think you can get me to waste time while I listen. I intend to win this race. I can pack and listen at the same time."

"We really should plan one mission named for St. Francis."

Galvez grunted. "Well, if St. Francis wants a mission, let him show us the place. Perhaps he can find us another bay like Monterey."

It had been years since any Spaniard had seen the beautiful Monterey Bay. Commandant Portola must try to find Monterey Bay. All he had were old maps to guide him.

Padre Serra took up his work again. "I believe that St. Francis will help us to find a bay even bigger and more beautiful than Monterey," he said. "We will name this bay San Francisco after St. Francis."

"I will remember that," Galvez said.

On January 11, 1769, the first ship, the San Carlos, set sail. The following month the San Antonio left. Next, the first part of the land expedition, under Captain Rivera, left on March 24. Padre Juan Crespi was with this group. He was happy that he would be working with Padre Serra again. Padre Serra and

Commandant Portola would leave a few weeks later. In time they would all meet in San Diego.

As Padre Serra traveled north, he stopped to say goodbye to many friends. He spent a few days with Padre Palou who was not going to Upper California. He had been appointed to take Padre Serra's place as head of the missions in Lower California.

"You look tired," Padre Palou told his old friend. "I wish you could stay here and that I could make the journey for you."

Padre Serra was much older now than when they first reached the New World. He was nearly fifty-six. Yet his eyes burned with enthusiasm.

"But, Francisco, this is what I have dreamed of. I might look tired now because of the extra work of preparation, but a few nights' rest will take care of that. Somehow I feel as though my life's work is just beginning. God has only been preparing me for the work to come. I am happier than I have ever been and stronger, too."

Padre Serra continued his journey north to the little mission of Guadalupe. There the padre in charge had a surprise for him. He introduced a young native American boy. He was small, but sturdy. The boy looked at Padre Serra shyly.

"This is Jose. He speaks Spanish as well as several dialects or languages that the native Americans use. He is very eager to join you on your adventure. He can be helpful when you meet new people and want to talk with them. He will translate for you and he can teach you the languages too."

Padre Serra smiled kindly. "How old are you,

Jose? You look so young. Perhaps you are too young for such a journey."

"I am fifteen," the boy answered, drawing himself up.

"Fifteen," repeated Padre Serra, surprised, and then he smiled. He remembered a time when he was so small that he was almost not allowed to become a Franciscan.

"You know, Jose, I have the feeling that before long you will grow very tall. I will be happy to have you as my companion and teacher."

The next day they set out early. When Jose grew tired, Padre Serra insisted that he ride on the mule that carried one of the mission bells. But Padre Serra himself always walked. His sandals made a soft, uneven sound on the path because he was limping badly.

At Velicata, the next settlement, they found Commandant Portola and the second part of the land expedition ready and waiting for them. In the morning after Mass and Holy Communion, the expedition set out for Upper California.

Padre Serra continued to walk, only now he was walking more slowly than ever. That night when he lay down to rest, he suddenly felt as if he could not get up again. When Commandant Portola came to see him, Padre Serra found that he could not even sit up.

"What is this?" demanded the commandant. "You are ill, Padre." Portola looked annoyed. "I knew it. I told Galvez that a lame friar would only cause trouble. And now I see I was right. What is to be done?"

"I am merely tired," Padre Serra said. "In the morning I will be fine."

"Nonsense!" said Commandant Portola. "You are ill, too ill to travel any more. I am sending you back to Velicata tomorrow."

Before Padre Serra could argue, the commandant waved his protests aside. "These are my orders. There is nothing more to be said."

He turned to go, but Padre Serra called after him in a firm, clear voice.

"It may not be God's will that I reach San Diego. I might die on the way, but I will not turn back."

Commandant Portola was not a man to have his orders ignored. Slowly he returned. For a moment he and Padre Serra looked hard at each other. Padre Serra was determined, but he knew that Commandant Portola could, if he chose, leave him behind. At last the commandant went on his way without speaking again. Padre Serra was worried.

The priest looked up at the clear night sky. If only there was something he could do about his leg. If only he could be on his feet and ready to go by morning. More than anything in the world he wanted to go to San Diego. He wanted to see this new land of Upper California and he wanted to meet the people there.

For a time he prayed, asking God to help him find a way to go on with his journey. Nearby Jose had long been asleep. He hadn't even heard what the commandant said. Nearly everyone else was asleep too. But Padre Serra was aware of the faint sound of whistling. Not far away a muleteer, a man who cared for the mules, was whistling softly to himself. The man was cheerful and good-natured. Padre Serra liked him.

"Juan," called Padre Serra, "can you come here a moment?"

At once the muleteer was beside him. "How can I help you, Padre? How are you feeling?"

"It's this troublesome leg of mine, Juan. I have been wondering. What do you do for a mule when it develops a sore like mine?"

The muleteer removed his wide-brimmed hat and ruffled his dark hair thoughtfully.

"Why, I make a hot bandage and place it on the wound. It is painful, but mules can bear that sort of thing. It is usually successful."

"Is it, Juan?" Padre Serra drew back his robe and showed the sore on his leg. "Do those sores look anything like this one?"

Juan gasped in surprise. "Oh, Padre. That is a mean one. But yes, I have seen such sores."

Padre Serra touched Juan's hand. "My son, I want you to pretend that I am one of your mules. Make a poultice for me."

"But, Padre, you can't mean it. The remedy is for animals. It would be too painful."

"Please, Juan. I need your help. I must be ready to go on with the expedition tomorrow. You are my one hope. Please."

After much pleading, Padre Serra convinced Juan to help him. The muleteer's hands trembled as he worked. Padre Serra made not a sound, though his leg hurt terribly. But at last the treatment was completed. Padre Serra was able to sleep.

Morning dawned bright and rosy. Men roused

themselves and prepared for another hard trip. Padre Serra opened his eyes to find little Jose bending over him.

"Good morning, Padre," Jose said. "Are you feeling better?"

Padre Serra moved his leg cautiously. It seemed to him the terrible swelling had gone down in the night. His leg hardly hurt at all. He sat up and then with Jose's help he was able to stand up. With great care he tested his leg by walking around their campfire. He was fine. God had answered his prayers.

At that moment Commandant Portola strode over, a look of amazement on his face.

Padre Serra smiled. "Jose and I are ready any time you are, Commandant."

Commandant Portola opened his mouth, closed it and finally spoke.

"Padre Serra," he said, "you are a most remarkable priest."

Padre Serra grinned broadly. "I am looking forward to our journey together."

7. Sergeant Ortega's Courage

The journey up the peninsula to Upper California was difficult. The trails were rough and much of the land was desert. But Padre Serra managed to be cheerful in spite of everything. His leg hardly bothered him at all.

Every morning he offered Mass and everyone in the expedition attended. Then they would travel doggedly until evening so they could sleep and get up the next morning to do the same thing all over again.

As they traveled, Padre Serra and the other friars made maps and named the places they passed.

Jose was puzzled. "Why do you bother, Padre Serra?" he asked. "The soldiers are making maps too and they give each place a different name. It is all very confusing."

This was true. The friars named various places after saints and famous Spaniards. The soldiers named places after incidents that occurred there. Once a soldier shot down a seagull, and they called that place Gaviota Pass or Seagull Pass. A place where a lame man was seen was called El Cojo, the Lame One, and so on.

"It is better to have too many names instead of

no name at all," Padre Serra told Jose. "The maps will help those who come after us. We are pioneers, Jose. We may be the first people to make any maps of this land at all."

One evening several men appeared on the hillside above their camp. "Look, there are some of the native Americans," said one of the soldiers.

Everyone stopped to watch them. It would be wonderful to be able to talk to these people.

"I count ten men and two boys," Sergeant Ortega said.

"We had better be careful. We don't know how many may be hiding nearby. If they are unfriendly, this could mean trouble," Commandant Portola said.

"They look friendly. Perhaps they are wondering if we are friendly too," Padre Serra said.

"Let me go to talk to them, Padre," Jose said. "I can tell them we are friends. I can invite them to meet you."

"You might be walking into danger," Commandant Portola said.

"I do not think so," Jose told him and off he went.

Minutes later he was back and smiling.

"They want to meet the padre. They have a gift for him, only it is not ready yet."

Portola frowned. "What sort of gift?"

"Wait and see," Jose said.

Not long afterward two people arrived. One was carrying a huge pancake on her head. When Padre Serra blessed her, she placed the sticky object in his hands. Everyone enjoyed a taste of the cake, but Commandant Portola was annoyed.

"Why are we wasting time eating cake?" he asked angrily.

"We have to be polite," Padre Serra said, his tone patient. "Our new friends were kind enough to give us a gift."

Portola shrugged disgustedly and stalked away.

"Padre, why does the commandant always talk like that?" Jose asked. "He sounds so angry all the time. I do not think he likes anyone at all."

Padre Serra put his arm on the boy's shoulder. "You must not take the commandant's behavior for dislike. He is a man with many responsibilities. All of us, even you and I, depend on him as our leader. I believe he speaks that way to hide his worries. He is a good man and he is concerned about us in this new land."

Once when Padre Serra was making friends with some native Americans, they pointed to his glasses. One woman wanted to examine the glasses more closely.

"So these glasses interest you, do they?" Padre Serra said. Without thinking, he handed his glasses to her. Seconds later she ran off, carrying the glasses. Because Padre Serra could not speak her language, she must have thought he had given them to her.

Poor Padre Serra! Here he was more than a thousand miles away from any place where he could get new glasses. It might be a year before he could get another pair.

"Jose, we must get those glasses back," he said. "You must explain that there has been a mistake."

Off they went. Here and there they met other native Americans and asked about the glasses. Jose used sign language, but he had no luck. No one knew anything about the glasses.

"We'd better give up, Padre."

But Padre Serra would not give up. He needed his glasses for reading, for saying Mass, for writing in his diary. He could not be without them. Up ahead he saw two women. One had something on her head that caught the light. The other seemed to be admiring this new ornament. As Padre Serra and Jose approached, they saw the woman who had gone off with the glasses. She was wearing them in her hair.

"Will she give them back?" Jose asked. "She might not want to give back a gift, especially one she likes so well. I'm not sure I can make her understand the mistake."

"I have an idea," said Padre Serra, drawing some colored beads from beneath his robe.

After many signs the woman seemed to understand. She liked the bright necklace and gave back the glasses.

That was quite an adventure, thought Padre Serra. After that he was more careful.

The trip grew more difficult every day. When the expedition party came to a desert, things went from bad to worse. The water supply was low and for a time it seemed they were lost.

Jose was discouraged. "I am afraid we will become food for the buzzards."

Padre Serra gave him a reproachful look. "Never give up hope, my son. Besides, today is the Feast of St. Anthony. Because St. Anthony was such a good man on earth, God grants him many favors in heaven.

Perhaps St. Anthony will ask God to help us out of our difficulties."

The very next morning scouts sent back word that they had found two water holes.

"When we reach this place, we will name it after the wonder-worker saint who helped us on this glorious day," one of the men decided.

But when the party of explorers did reach the water holes, the animals swarmed around them and drank all the water. There was hardly any left for cooking.

"We should call this place San Antonio of the Hardships, I think," Jose said.

Padre Serra was sorry about the disappointment, but he was still hopeful.

That evening the scouts came back with good news.

"Water, two beautiful streams, only a day away!"

The news spread quickly. The men shouted and threw their hats in the air.

"We have passed through the desert. There are green pastures and water ahead," they said.

But the journey was far from over. Many of the soldiers were unhappy. They quarreled among themselves. The land soon grew rough again. The party was climbing rocky mountain trails. Cliffs fell away so sharply that everyone was in constant danger of slipping and falling. Padre Serra saw Jose eyeing the heavy mission bell. Perhaps he wished they could leave it behind.

Traveling was very slow. The men were able to

do little more than crawl most of the time. At last the journey became so difficult that the men refused to go on.

"How do we know what is ahead? Perhaps we are hopelessly lost and will never find San Diego. Let us go back before it is too late," they begged.

Angrily, Commandant Portola forced the men to go on, but Padre Serra knew it would not be long before some of them decided to run away in the night.

It was the young Sergeant Ortega who brought hope to the expedition.

"Let me go ahead. I'll take one man with me. We shall see for ourselves what is beyond the mountains."

Commandant Portola agreed, and the sergeant came for Padre Serra's blessing.

"You are very brave, my son. *Vaya con Dios.* Go with God and bring back good news," he said.

While Sergeant Ortega was gone, Commandant Portola forced his men forward. Everyone worried about the valiant soldier who had gone to scout ahead. Day after day they hoped for his return.

Five days later the men heard a shout from a hilltop. It was Sergeant Ortega. Padre Serra offered a silent prayer of thanksgiving.

Sergeant Ortega had not yet found San Diego Bay, but he had found signs that they were very close. The end of the journey was near.

At last, on July 1, 1769, Sergeant Ortega led the tired men to a place where they could finally see the Pacific Ocean. The land curved inland in a huge half-circle. This was San Diego Bay. There, riding at anchor, were the two ships that had gone ahead of the land party.

The men set up a tremendous shout of joy. Padre Serra knelt down and kissed the earth. A glorious song of praise filled his heart.

When he stood up, he saw Jose watching him fondly.

"Well, Padre?" Jose said.

"Well, Jose?" Padre Serra asked with a twinkle in his eye. "Aren't you glad we did not leave the mission bell behind?"

"You knew!" Jose said, looking embarrassed.

"I knew."

"I am very glad I was wrong," Jose admitted. "I will be happy to help you hang the bell in the bell tower as soon as we build it."

8. St. Joseph's Miracle

Commandant Portola's gun salute boomed through the stillness to signal the first band of explorers that the second land party had arrived. Shouts and cries of welcome reached the tired group of soldiers and missionaries. Then an answering gun salute echoed through the mountains. Soon members of Captain Rivera's band rushed to meet their valiant comrades. It was July 1, 1769. For forty days Portola's party had been on the march from Velicata.

Padre Juan Crespi greeted Padre Serra.

"We worried. We prayed. And now you are here. Thanks be to God," he cried.

After the happiness of seeing friends again came some grim facts.

"We have had a great deal of trouble," Captain Rivera reported. "Our men are sick. The captain and crew of the San Carlos, except for one sailor and the cook, are dead. The crew members of the San Antonio are also very ill. Neither ship is in any condition to go on to find Monterey. Besides this, our supplies are low."

"Well, Captain, there is no point in thinking about our misfortunes. We must be thankful for what we have. Today we will rest. Tomorrow we will decide what to do," Portola said.

The next morning Padre Serra celebrated a Mass of thanksgiving. Then the leaders met to discuss what must be done. Commandant Portola was no longer gruff when he spoke to Padre Serra.

Padre Serra was pleased that the commandant no longer thought of him as a nuisance. There was respect in the soldier's eyes as he asked Padre Serra what he thought should be done first.

"We must do what we can for the sick," Padre Serra said. "And we must find a way to build the mission of San Diego."

Commandant Portola agreed. "We must also find Monterey Bay before the Russians decide to come down and build their own settlements. Then Spain will lose its claim to California. What are we to do about that?"

Suggestions were made. At last the men came up with a plan. Padre Serra, Padre Parron and Padre Vizcaino would remain at San Diego. A few soldiers would stay with them. Here the sick would be nursed to health. The friars who stayed behind would build the mission of San Diego.

As soon as a few men could be gathered together from among the healthy, the San Antonio would go back to Lower California. Their ship could bring back new crews for herself and for the San Carlos along with the desperately needed supplies. In the meantime Commandant Portola, with Captain Rivera and

Padre Juan Crespi, would go north by land in search of the lost Monterey Bay.

The plan was put into action at once. Commandant Portola gathered his men and started on his journey. The remaining soldiers set about building huts and a fence or palisade to protect the mission, just in case some of the native Americans were not friendly. One of the huts was set aside to be used as a temporary church. This is how the mission of San Diego began.

The padres set up a large cross outdoors within sight of the sea. Jose gathered boughs for the roof of the hut and the soldiers chopped down trees for the chapel walls. It was a rough building, but it was the first mission in Upper California. Padre Serra thought it was beautiful.

"All right, Jose. Bring the bell," he said.

Proudly the boy led the little mule that had carried the bell all the way from Lower California. The bell was hung on the bough of a tree because they did not have a bell tower.

The moment the bell was secure, Padre Serra pulled on the rope. The voice of the bell carried clearly through the morning air. It floated out over the harbor. It rang over the land and sounded far into the hills and surrounding woods. It sounded wonderful. Someday the bell would call people to Mass.

The next thing Padre Serra and the friars had to do was to learn the language of the local tribe of native Americans. Soon they were able to talk with their new neighbors.

As always, the children became especially fond

of Padre Serra. He learned their greeting and they learned his. "Amad a Dios," Padre Serra liked to say instead of "hello." The Spanish words mean "Love God."

Not all of the new neighbors were friendly, though. On August 15, after Padre Parron had gone to the ship to say Mass, there were only four soldiers, two friars and Jose left at the mission. Padre Serra said Mass in the chapel. When he rang the bell that morning, some members of the local tribe came to Mass too.

Then without warning the little mission was attacked. A band of angry men swooped down on them, shouting and shooting their arrows. The fence the friars had built was no protection at all. The men simply knocked it down. The four soldiers who were still at the mission fired their guns into the air. This did not frighten the enemy away. The padres went to Padre Serra's hut for safety. Jose helped barricade the opening as best he could. All the while, frenzied yells pierced the air. The mission was in serious trouble.

Jose's hands shook with fear as he pulled the last board across the doorway. Padre Serra spoke calmly. "All will be well. God is watching over us."

Jose looked up at Padre Serra. "I believe you," he said. "I am being foolish and cowardly. The soldiers will need someone to load their guns. I will go to help them."

Before anyone could stop him, Jose rushed out, replacing the board as he left.

The friars knelt in prayer as a shower of arrows fell on the hut. No one knew why this group of native Americans was so angry or why they wanted to destroy the mission. Although the number of soldiers there was small, their guns and the deadly explosions frightened the enemy. At last they retreated.

As the sound of their shouting faded, Padre Vizcaino reached up and lifted the barricade. But the enemy had not given up entirely. An arrow pierced the priest's hand.

At the same time there was a painful cry outside. Padre Serra recognized Jose's voice. He ran to the doorway. His heart sank as the boy fell into his arms. An arrow had struck him in the throat. A few moments later he died.

Suddenly every misfortune that had befallen the explorers weighed heavily on Padre Serra. He thought of the men who were still sick. He thought of the lost Bay of Monterey and the need for new supplies. And now Jose had died at the hands of the very people he wanted to teach about God. Some of the soldiers were wounded too.

"Why did we come?" they grumbled. "These people don't want us here. What is the point of building a mission now?"

After that the soldiers worked only half-heartedly. Padre Serra himself was discouraged. Every day he prayed for faith. Every day he hoped there would be some sign that all their hardships had not been in vain.

And then out of the tragedy came an unexpected victory. Some of the band of raiders who were wounded by the soldiers' bullets came to the mission for help. The friars were surprised, but they welcomed these men and took care of their wounds.

The native Americans were grateful. The children told Padre Serra that the men never would have treated an enemy so kindly.

Padre Serra thought this was a turning point. The native Americans were at last beginning to trust the Spaniards. They realized that the padres meant them no harm. Men and women began to come to the mission as regularly as the children.

The missionaries were able to solve most of the difficulties at San Diego, but, far to the north, the land expedition was searching for the oval Bay of Monterey. Unknowingly they had wandered too far north and they missed Monterey.

Instead, the soldiers made an important discovery which they did not recognize at the time. Reaching a rise of ground, some of the soldiers looked out at a magnificent sight. The waters of the Pacific sparkled brilliantly in the clear air as they flowed between a golden gateway of land. To the north, the shore curved and the water flowed inland, forming a little cove.

This magnificent bay was not what the explorer Vizcaino described as Monterey Bay. This was much bigger and far more glorious. They named it San Francisco Bay.

When Commandant Portola, Padre Crespi and the men returned to San Diego Bay on January 24, 1770, they told what they had found.

Padre Serra knew the men were discouraged. He didn't blame them. But he felt the explorers had found something far more valuable and he was happy.

"I knew St. Francis would help us find a place for his own mission," he said.

When Commandant Portola learned all that had happened at the mission in his absence, the military leader was very concerned. The San Antonio had not yet returned with supplies. The little band of Spaniards could not hold out much longer. The commandant waited two months and then went to Padre Serra.

"We have to give up," he said. "I am sorry for your sake and for my own, but if we don't go back to Mexico, everyone will die."

"Surely we can wait a while longer. We have suffered so much," argued Padre Serra. "You have always been courageous. How can we give up?"

The commandant shook his head. "Padre, I know you are a stubborn man, but I am stubborn too. In this I know I am right."

Padre Serra could see it would be hard to change this man's mind. Still, he tried.

"Commandant, grant me one favor. It is March 10. In nine days it will be the Feast of St. Joseph. Let us pray for nine days. If the San Antonio does not come back by March 19, I too will admit defeat. Please."

Padre Serra looked at the commandant with steady eyes in which the light of his faith burned brightly. Portola looked away.

He sighed. "Very well, but we cannot wait longer than that."

For nine days the missionaries and the men prayed, but the ship did not come. By St. Joseph's Day the soldiers were packed and ready to leave. When evening came, Portola went to Padre Serra in the chapel.

"I am sorry, Padre. I know how hard you have

prayed and how much San Diego means to you, but I do not think there is any reason to hope that the San Antonio will come now."

He stood in the doorway, his hat in his hand. Padre Serra bowed his head. He was no longer young. He knew if he left San Diego, he would never return. If a new expedition were organized, a younger man would be appointed president of the missions. This would be the end of his dream.

But Padre Serra straightened his shoulders. He was not ready to give up hope.

"St. Joseph's Day is not yet over, Commandant."

Quietly the two men left the chapel and climbed the hill where a hopeful band of men was watching for the San Antonio. Everyone was silent. That morning they had sung Mass in honor of St. Joseph. Hour after hour they waited. The sun was going down and a rosy sunset tinted the sky. Then as the light was fading, a dark speck no bigger than a fly came into view. The men began to point and shout. Could it be? They waited a little longer. No, there was no mistake.

"A sail, a sail!" someone shouted.

"A sail, a sail!" the cry went up and spread through the camp.

"The San Antonio has come. Praise be to God!" cried the friars.

"A miracle, a miracle!" exclaimed the men in awed voices.

Padre Serra fell to his knees. Their prayers had been answered. The work of the missions would continue and he would be part of it.

9. Padre Serra's Victory

What a change the coming of the San Antonio brought! Only a day before the explorers and the missionaries had been in deep despair. Now their hearts were filled with hope.

Surely the tasks of exploration and founding settlements in the New World were especially blessed. They fell to work with enthusiasm again. Captain Perez of the San Antonio even had an idea about how to find Monterey Bay.

"The maps you were using were made over a hundred and fifty years ago," he told Commandant Portola. "Probably they are not very accurate. It seems to me that you overshot your mark. Let us try again. I will sail up the coast and you can go by land. With both of us searching in that way, we cannot fail."

"This is a good plan," Portola said. "I feel so sure we can be successful that this time, Father President, you should come with us. What do you say? Only I think you should travel by sea. It will give your leg a chance to rest and heal altogether."

Padre Serra thought for a moment. The sooner they found Monterey Bay and established the mis-

sion, the better. Very probably the ship would reach Monterey first.

"Very well," he agreed. "I will be waiting for you at Monterey, Commandant. You can be the first travelers to hear Mass at Mission San Carlos."

Padre Parron and Padre Gomez were left in charge of San Diego. Padre Crespi accompanied Portola with the land expedition.

The ocean voyage was not as easy as Padre Serra expected. The trip took more than six weeks. He spent his time writing letters and worrying about the land expedition. How were they doing? Were they lost again? He wondered how long he would have to wait at Monterey for the explorers to join them there.

Later he learned that the trip by land was much easier and faster. It was spring. The hills were covered with wild fruits and flowers. One evening when the party set up their camp, the leaders sat down to discuss their position. The soldiers went exploring on their own.

Suddenly Commandant Portola heard his men shouting. He thought these men had been hunting and were excited about capturing a strange animal.

But when the commotion did not die down, Commandant Portola and the other leaders rushed to see what had happened.

"The bay!" the men were shouting. "The bay! Monterey is found."

The soldiers led their leaders over a little hill. There lay the curved bay of glittering sapphire water along the dazzling white shore. It was a breathtaking sight.

"I can hardly believe it," Portola exclaimed.

"How close we came before without seeing it! How blind we were!"

On June 3, 1770, the San Antonio docked at the Bay of Monterey, guided by the fires built by the soldiers to act as signals on the shore. An altar was set up the next day under an oak near the bay where Mass had been said by the Spaniards one hundred and fifty years before when Monterey had first been discovered. The mission bells were hung. A cross and the King's royal standard were erected. Padre Serra sang the Mass. In a joyous ceremony Commandant Portola officially took possession of the land for Spain.

The soldiers fired a salute. From the bay the San Antonio answered. Portola had carried out his mission successfully. Now he could return to Mexico in triumph.

But Padre Serra's work would now begin in earnest. Portola left and a new military commander was appointed in his place. This was Don Pedro Fages. At once Padre Serra could see that this man was different from the honorable Portola. Whenever he could, Fages managed to disagree with the friars.

"Perhaps it would be best to build our mission some distance away from where the soldiers are staying. That way we can avoid arguments," Padre Serra said.

The soldiers always stayed in their own quarters, which was called the presidio, near the missions. This time Padre Serra went three miles away to the banks of the Carmel River. There he and the friars built their Mission of San Carlos. Slowly it took shape. There were long low buildings of yellow mud brick. With his own hands Padre Serra helped with the work. In the central court he placed a large wooden cross. Here he spent many hours in prayer.

The climate of Carmel was warm and pleasant the year round. The surroundings were beautiful. This place reminded Padre Serra so much of his home in Majorca that he decided the Mission of San Carlos would be his headquarters. The mission was opened in December 1771.

Within a few days' journey of Carmel was the mission dedicated to San Antonio. The land around the mission was blessed with fertile soil. Farms here produced fine crops. This mission grew more rapidly than any of the others. San Gabriel Mission was built about nine miles from the place where the city of Los Angeles stands today. Between there and San Antonio, Padre Serra planned to build San Luis Obispo.

El Camino Real was taking shape just the way Padre Serra had planned. There were five missions at which travelers might stop along the Royal Road. Someday there would be a continuous chain of missions up and down the coast within a day's walking journey of one another.

New missionaries were pouring into Upper California. The missionaries made friends with the native Americans.

But the hardships were not over. In 1772 a terrible famine struck. Some of the native Americans began to build their huts near the missions. They wanted to become farmers. Until this time they had never farmed before. They found food by hunting wild game and by eating roots and berries. With the padres' help these people planted grain. But by summer the wheat was not ready to harvest. Food was scarce and everyone was suffering.

"What can we do, Padre Serra?" one of the friars asked. "We have hardly enough flour to last one week. There is no meat. Can we send to Mexico for supplies?"

"By the time the supplies reached us, we would starve," Padre Serra said. "We will have to ration our food. A little corn, flour and milk each day will have to do until we can find other food. I will speak to Commandant Fages."

Padre Serra did not like to speak to Fages at all. He did not expect to find him helpful. But he went directly to see the commandant.

"Could your men organize a hunting party? Until the autumn harvest, we will have little food," Padre Serra said.

"A hunting party!" exclaimed the commandant scornfully. "What shall we hunt—rabbits?"

"Even rabbits would be a welcome sight," replied Padre Serra. For a moment he thought that the commandant would refuse to help, but even Fages saw that the situation was desperate.

"Well," he said, "I have heard the men say that there is a valley near here where a large number of bears have been seen. We will hunt bears."

Fages and his men remained in the Valley of the Bears for more than two months. They sent back meat regularly. At the mission the commandant became a great hero. But he was not a hero to his men.

The soldiers considered him unreasonable and unnecessarily strict. They complained to the friars.

When Padre Serra tried to warn Fages that his men would desert if he did not treat them more fairly, the commandant only became angry.

Finally many soldiers did desert the camp. They went into the hills to live and only returned when the missionaries begged them to come back.

In October 1772, Padre Serra was in San Diego. He had walked all the way from Monterey. On the way he stopped to start a new mission called San Luis Obispo.

At San Diego he had bad news from his missionaries.

"Something must be done," the friars told him. "Commandant Fages is even standing in the way of our founding new missions. He does not ask for the necessary soldiers, animals and supplies to be sent from Mexico."

Padre Serra was sitting at his writing desk in his small room when the missionaries came to see him. The tiny room contained only a desk and the wooden slab where he slept. Padre Junipero Serra was nearly fifty-nine years old. His lame leg had never healed properly and there were tired lines in his face. Yet he was as determined as he had always been to make the missions a success. Only minutes before he had finished a letter to the man who was the head of the Spanish settlements in the New World. He was the viceroy who was stationed in Mexico City. Padre Serra asked him for help.

He sighed when the missionaries told him their problems.

"I suppose a letter is not the answer. I have

written many letters to the viceroy and have received no answer. I am afraid that I must go to see Viceroy Antonio Bucareli myself."

"But it is such a long journey," Padre Dumetz said. "You should take things easier now."

Padre Serra smiled. "I think that I was never meant to have an easy life. After all, we did not become missionaries because we wanted to take it easy."

On October 20, 1772, Padre Serra took the ship to San Blas, Mexico. From there he walked to Guadalajara. Twice he fell ill with fever and twice he recovered. Finally he arrived in Mexico City where he went to see Viceroy Bucareli. The viceroy listened to all Padre Serra told him.

"It would seem we must replace the commandant," he said. "If this is what I decide, Padre, is there someone you would recommend?"

Padre Serra did not have to think twice. He remembered the courage of Sergeant Ortega who had saved the land expedition by scouting the wilderness on that first trip from Mexico to Upper California. This was his choice.

"He is the best military man I know," Padre Serra said.

"Yes, but he is young," said the viceroy, "perhaps too young. But I will consider him."

Padre Serra had to wait several months for an answer, but the waiting was worth it. The viceroy gave the Father President everything he wanted. New orders were given for building the missions at San Francisco and San Buenaventura. Commandant Fages was recalled and Captain Rivera was to take his place. Although this was not Padre Serra's choice, it meant progress and he thanked the viceroy.

"If you really want to thank me, you will obey my orders. Your stubbornness is legend. I have ordered a coach to carry you back to Guadalajara. You have been ill and I have consulted your superiors about this. There will be no arguments."

Padre Serra returned to Mission San Carlos and only walked part of the way. It was two years since he had left. He was hopeful that now the mission work would run smoothly.

10. *The Missions' First Martyr*

Padre Serra was anxious to reach San Carlos. He knew that a very old friend would be there waiting for him. When they were face to face, he saw that Padre Palou was older and thinner, but he still had the same happy smile.

"Francisco! I'm so glad to see you. Tell me all your news."

It had been so long since the friends had been together that they hardly stopped talking for a moment. Dominican missionaries had now taken over the missions in Lower California. While Padre Serra had been in Mexico, Francisco Palou had been sent up to San Carlos to act in the Father President's place. The Franciscans were no longer needed in Lower California.

"We don't have to make up for all the years in one hour," said Padre Palou finally. "We can save some more talk for tomorrow and the day after that."

Padre Serra laughed. He was happy. Together he and Padre Palou would complete the building of the missions without any trouble at all.

What Padre Serra did not know was that trouble

was brewing in San Diego where Padre Luis Jayme was in charge. In the autumn of 1775, the harvest was good and more and more native Americans were coming to the mission to live and to learn about Our Lord.

Sergeant Ortega, who was now a lieutenant and part of the group of soldiers assigned to protect the mission, was concerned about two of the native Americans who lived there. They were Joachin and Francisco. Even Padre Jayme thought these men were strangely quiet. They seldom spoke to anyone but each other. One day Joachin and Francisco left the mission and did not come back.

"What could have happened?" said Padre Fuster.

"Perhaps they have gone to bring some of their friends and relatives to join us," said Padre Jayme.

But Padre Fuster was worried. He wished he could talk over this problem with Padre Serra. He thought that Joachin and Francisco were not happy. Some of the other men and women at the mission said that these two men thought the padres had come to make slaves of them instead of coming to teach them about God. Joachin and Francisco forgot how often their tribe had been without food before the padres came and showed them how to farm and store crops. They forgot how many of their tribe had died before the padres brought them medicine and helped make them well.

On the night of November 5, 1775, Joachin and Francisco did return. But they were not alone. They brought a large war party of nearly a thousand men. The party waited until some of the soldiers left to help open another mission. With only a handful of soldiers at the presidio, the mission was poorly guarded.

Everyone slept peacefully beneath the clear, moonlit sky. Posting armed guards around the living quarters so that no one could escape, the band of men began their destructive work. Silently they stole into the church and tore down the statues and the altar. They carried away the vestments.

They threw fireballs at the thatched roofs of the buildings. Too late the sleepers awoke. Unfortunately the soldiers at the presidio did not see the fire at the mission in time to send help. The blaze went unnoticed at first because of the strong moonlight that night.

"May God have mercy on us. We are lost," cried Padre Fuster.

Padre Jayme stood up resolutely. "Perhaps the men will listen to me," he said. "I must try."

The young missionary stepped bravely outside.

"Amad a Dios, mis hijos," he said in a loud voice, just as Padre Serra used to do. "Love God, my children."

It was the last thing the other padres heard him say. The missionaries huddled inside their hut.

A furious battle raged for hours. One of the blacksmiths was killed at once. A young corporal held the enemy off with deadly marksmanship. When at last the attackers had gone, it was nearly morning and the mission was destroyed.

Everyone looked for Padre Jayme. At last they found him. He had been killed. The padres said he was a martyr. They buried him in the chapel because the church had been burned to the ground.

When news of the attack on the San Diego mission reached Commandant Rivera, he was very angry. He and his men hurried to San Diego where they searched out the leaders of the attack. One of the men returned to the chapel and asked for forgiveness.

Now it is the rule of the Church that anyone who seeks safety in a Catholic church may not be removed by force. The padres wanted to forgive this native American who said he was sorry. But Commandant Rivera would not let them do this.

"Ridiculous!" he shouted. "I will not forgive him, and I don't think you can call this ruined chapel a church."

The soldiers dragged the man away to prison. The padres could do nothing to stop Rivera.

When Padre Serra arrived in San Diego, he was faced with many problems again. He found that Rivera was planning to send the leaders of the attack back to San Blas in Mexico for punishment. Padre Serra thought this was a terrible mistake.

"Release these men to the missionaries," he said. "We can help them. They are sorry for what they have done."

"Never," said Rivera. "They are criminals and must be punished as criminals."

Finally Padre Serra had to give up. Instead, he turned his attention to rebuilding the mission.

"Why has so little been done?" he asked.

"There is no one to help us. Rivera will give us none of his men to help. The work goes very slowly," explained one of the padres.

Padre Serra was beginning to think Commandant

Rivera was every bit as bad as Commandant Fages. But then he had an idea.

The San Antonio had sailed into the harbor. Padre Serra went to see his old friend Captain Diego Choquet.

"Diego, I need your help. Will you and your men help rebuild the mission of your own patron saint?" he asked.

Captain Choquet was flattered. "Certainly we will help. I think my men can do a fine job and the fastest one you ever saw."

The work began at once, but when Commandant Rivera found out about it, he was angry. One day he rode over to speak with Captain Choquet.

"I think you should be warned, Captain," Rivera said.

"Warned? What do you mean?"

"We have heard that there might be another attack," said Rivera. "You are in danger."

Captain Choquet looked him in the eye. "Why, Commandant," he said boldly, "if you are so worried about our safety, why don't you provide us with more guards?"

Angry and embarrassed, Rivera rode away. But he did have his way. Captain Choquet and his men were forced to stop. They were recalled to San Blas before they had finished their work.

Padre Serra was not about to give up. Mission San Diego was the first link of his chain of missions. It must be rebuilt. He wrote to the viceroy in Mexico City and asked for permission to rebuild the mission. At last he had an answer. The viceroy approved of this work and ordered the soldiers to help. Soon

Commandant Rivera was recalled to Lower California. The viceroy sent Governor Felipe de Neve to go to Monterey and see personally to the progress of the missions. Now El Camino Real, the Royal Road, grew rapidly.

For some time Padre Serra wanted to build missions north of Monterey.

"How long our father St. Francis has had to wait for his mission!" he said many times.

Finally Captain Anza arrived from Mexico with orders to select a place for a mission and a presidio for the soldiers near the excellent harbor of San Francisco. Padre Serra was so busy at San Diego that Padre Palou was sent to found Mission San Francisco de Asis. A rough chapel was set up and the bell hung. Today the bell is still rung in the mission which stands in the heart of the beautiful city of San Francisco that grew up around it. Padre Palou erected the cross and blessed the site on October 9, 1776.

The mission of San Juan Capistrano was refounded. It had first been established a few days before the attack on San Diego. When news of the attack reached San Juan Capistrano, the soldiers left at once to help in San Diego and the friars accompanied them. The Capistrano mission bell had been buried. Now it was recovered and ready to be hung properly.

North of Monterey, building began on the mission of Santa Clara. It was completed on January 12, 1777.

On Easter Sunday in 1782, Padre Serra founded San Buenaventura. It was the last of the golden chain of missions that stretched along El Camino Real that he would establish himself. It was San Buenaventura for which Inspector General Galvez had been packing when he raced with Padre Serra so long ago.

The years went by and Padre Serra grew older. He felt that soon God would call him. In the summer of 1783, he decided to make the rounds of his nine missions one last time.

Everywhere he went the friars were glad to see him, but saddened by his weary appearance. During the past few years Padre Serra had developed a bad case of asthma. He was very ill. But this did not keep him from traveling.

From San Diego he went to San Juan Capistrano and San Gabriel, and then on to San Buenaventura. He traveled to San Luis Obispo, San Antonio and home to San Carlos. Here he stayed during Lent and celebrated Easter before continuing. At Santa Clara he blessed the new church.

When he arrived at San Francisco, how glad Padre Palou was to see him! Unfortunately they did not have much time together, for the padre in charge of Santa Clara was ill. Padre Palou had to leave for that mission and Padre Serra followed later.

At home in San Carlos Padre Serra sat down to write farewell messages to all the missions. To Padre Palou he sent an urgent message to come to him at once. Worried, his old friend arrived in a hurry.

"Well, now that I am here, I shall see to it that you rest," Padre Palou told Padre Serra. "I don't expect to have any arguments either, because I am not afraid to point out that I am bigger than you are."

For once Padre Serra did not argue.

11. The Golden Highway

Padre Serra stretched himself after his night's rest. It was nearly daybreak and the soft light of dawn found its way through the little window into his tiny room. He drew his one rough blanket neatly over his narrow wooden bed and set out for the church to say the first Mass of the day.

He walked very slowly, for his leg was troubling him. Sometimes it was difficult for him to breathe. He paused in prayer before the large wooden cross in the courtyard. There was a great deal of pain in his chest this morning, but he paid little attention to it.

When the mission bells began to sound their morning call, he looked up and smiled to see the birds fly hurriedly out of the belfry. They had been rudely frightened from their home.

Two altar boys met him at the church. "Good morning, Padre," they greeted him. One of them stared solemnly with his dark eyes upon the old missionary's face.

"Are you feeling better this morning?" he asked.

"I am not ill. Do not look so worried or you will convince me that I am, little one," said Padre Serra cheerfully.

At Mass that morning Padre Serra had a fit of coughing. But afterward he felt better and called some children together to tell them stories that helped them understand the rules of the Church.

Padre Palou found him there. "Padre Junipero," he said, "there you are. I was worried. Your altar boys told me you were ill at Mass. Why aren't you resting?"

"Francisco, you should know by now that I cannot sit idly by while there is work to be done," said Padre Serra, and he went right ahead with the lesson.

The children were pleased to have the old padre teach them. They leaned against him and clasped his hands, gazing into his loving face while he told stories of Jesus.

But the next day Padre Serra was so sick that he stayed in his room.

Two days later he told Padre Palou he wanted to receive Communion.

"I will come to the church to receive it," Padre Serra said.

"But that isn't necessary," protested Padre Palou. "We will bring Communion to you."

"As long as I can walk to the church, there is no need for Our Lord to come to me. I will go to Him," insisted Padre Serra.

Kneeling in the little wooden church before the altar of Our Lady, Padre Serra received Our Lord for the last time. The church glowed with the light of the candles held by the soldiers and by the native Americans who lived at the mission. Padre Serra looked around him and saw that his friends looked very sad. He wanted to tell them that they should not be sad for him. Soon God, his Father, would call him, and Padre Serra was ready to go. He felt that his heavenly Father was pleased with the work he had done. Padre Serra had certainly tried his best.

He wished he could tell his friends how happy he was to be going to God, but he was too weak to say anything. Instead, he kept all these things in his heart. He went back to his bed and did not get up again.

The next afternoon he whispered to Padre Palou that he would go on praying for the missions. He asked Padre Palou to carry on his work.

Then he smiled and closed his eyes. Perhaps Padre Junipero Serra was thinking about the small boy he had once been. Little Miguel Serra had accomplished things he would never have dreamed of. Lame and no longer young, Padre Serra had started on a long and difficult road in the New World.

Along the way men had been discouraged. Some had turned back and given up. But Padre Serra never gave up. He knew a valuable secret. He knew that with God's help even a little lame friar could be as big as anyone else inside. Padre Serra's lips curved in a faint smile and he breathed his last.

It was Padre Palou's sad duty to tell everyone that Padre Junipero Serra had died. Mournfully the mission bell tolled. Men, women and children stood about weeping. They would miss the gentle padre very much.

That Sunday, after a long procession, Padre Serra's body was laid to rest in the Church of San Carlos in the sanctuary on the Gospel side.

For many weeks the people of the mission felt

sad and lonely. They were like sheep who had lost their shepherd. Some of them went to Padre Palou.

"Is there something I can have—any little thing that I can keep near me to remember Padre Serra?"

Padre Serra had few belongings, but Padre Palou gave these people what little he could find: a piece of a tunic, a handkerchief, a book.

Not long afterward stories of unusual incidents connected with these objects reached Padre Palou. He had sent one of Padre Serra's handkerchiefs to the royal physician. The doctor sent this report to Padre Palou.

"One of my men was suffering with terrible headaches that made him so ill he could not sleep. Nothing I could do helped. Then I fastened Padre Serra's handkerchief about this man's head. When he woke in the morning, the pain was gone."

Padre Palou kept this report because he thought it was most remarkable. Then Padre Palou witnessed another incident himself. Padre Paterno had been on his way to see Padre Serra, but arrived too late. The funeral was already over. This friar was an older man, and the heat of August weakened him so that he became very ill.

"Would you like me to give you Padre Serra's shirt to wear?" asked Padre Palou.

Padre Paterno accepted this gratefully. It wasn't long before he was completely well.

Padre Palou began to wonder if these were miraculous cures that revealed Padre Serra as one of God's saints. He began to collect these stories and all he knew about Padre Serra in a book. He wrote to his superiors and told them what he thought. Soon news of the little friar and all the wonderful things he had done reached Rome.

Work was begun to study the life of Padre Serra. It took many years. Long after Padre Palou died, men studied the stories he had written about Padre Serra. The Church Fathers in Rome looked carefully at all the information they could find about Padre Serra and all the good work he had done. They studied the many stories of miracles connected with the little lame friar.

Padre Serra died on August 28, 1784. Two hundred and four years later, on May 4, 1988, the Church announced that an important step would be taken. In a ceremony at Mass in St. Peter's Basilica, Padre Serra was to beatified on September 25, 1988. Padre Serra was then only one step away from being declared one of God's saints.

UNITED
STATES

UPPER
CALIFORNIA

SAN FRANCISCO
de ASIS
• SANTA CLARA

• CARMEL

SAN ANTONIO
de PADUA

• SAN LUIS OBISPO

• SAN BUENAVENTURA
• SAN GABRIEL

SAN JUAN
CAPISTRANO

SAN DIEGO

PACIFIC
OCEAN

• VELICATA

• GUADALUPE

LA PURISIMA •

LORETO •

SAN FRANCISCO
XAVIER

• LA PAZ

LOWER
CALIFORNIA

MEXICO

SAN BLAS • • TEPIC

GUADALAJARA •

• JALPAN

• QUERETARO

VERA CRUZ

MEXICO CITY ○

PACIFIC
OCEAN

Epilogue

The people of California have long recognized Padre Junipero Serra's contribution to the history of their state and to our country.

In 1927, the Congress of the United States decided to set up memorials in Washington, D.C. to honor the founding fathers of our nation. They asked the people of each of the then forty-eight states to name two favorite state heroes. One of those chosen by Californians was Padre Junipero Serra.

On March 1, 1931, at 3 o'clock in the afternoon, a group of senators, representatives and honored guests gathered in Statuary Hall in the Capitol Building in Washington, D.C. There the statue of Junipero Serra was presented and unveiled.

The Honorable Isidore Bernard Dockweiler, a California attorney who had devoted much of his time following the example of Junipero Serra by working on behalf of native Americans, gave an address honoring Padre Serra.

Dockweiler ended his speech with these words:

"His (Serra's) inextinguishable mark is upon the face of California. He is California's apostle to the Indians. He is our country's first civilizer of our western coast. He justly stands, for the edification of future generations, among the immortals of our Nation.

"It was of such men as this, that Solomon in all his wisdom, sang—'His memory shall not recede, and his name shall be looked for from generation to generation.' "